SPEAK
FOR
YOURSELF

About the Author

Richard Denny is one of the UK's foremost authorities on sales, management training and personal development.

He commenced his working life in agriculture and then diversified into the selling and marketing of a diverse range of products, from foodstuffs to cement, detergents to electronic watches, both in the UK and abroad.

He is currently Chairman of his own group of companies, producing video training programmes, audio cassette libraries and tailor-made courses. He also acts as a consultant and retained advisor to some key UK multinationals.

As a speaker he has an unparalleled reputation for his motivational presentations. Since 1976 he has averaged some 170 personal appearances each year. Richard Denny has the uncanny ability of inspiring people to greater achievement. He claims not to be a theoretician but a practitioner.

Married with 5 sons, his home and office are in the Cotswolds.

SPEAK
FOR
YOURSELF

**Tested Techniques
for Improving Your
Communication
and Presentation
Skills**

J. S. Andrader

28.6.94

RICHARD DENNY

**KOGAN
PAGE**

First published in 1994

Kogan Page Limited
120 Pentonville Road
London N1 9JN

©Richard Denny, 1994

British Library Cataloguing in Publication Data

A CIP record for this book is available from the British Library.

ISBN 0 7494 0963 0 (Hardback) 0 7494 0964 9 (Paperback)

Typeset by Books Unlimited (Nottm), Sutton-in-Ashfield, NG17 AL
Printed in England by Clays Ltd, St Ives plc

Contents

For Linda, my beautiful wife and business partner.

Debbie Poulter. Your were great. Thank you once again for your enthusiasm and, of course, your speed and agility with the computer.

Preface

You have probably begged, borrowed, stolen or purchased (I hope) this book because the title appealed to you. If that is true, excellent. This is a book written for those who would really like to be a better and more persuasive communicator. It is about getting your own point of view across to whoever the message is directed at.

It is based upon speaking as a function of communicating to numbers of people rather than to the individual, but the messages, tips, advice and ideas in most cases are exactly the same.

If you never see yourself speaking or communicating in public, still read on. If you do see yourself having to communicate in public, you are holding a valuable aid.

Introduction

I don't believe anybody was born a gifted public speaker and public speaking is not some mystical art whose skills a chosen few have been fortunate enough to inherit. There is almost nothing that instils so much fear in people as having to stand up and speak in public.

I recall during my years of farming in Sussex attending various meetings and dinner-jacket events with guest speakers. There were toasts to this or that and the inevitable vote of thanks. I sat through these occasions dreading, with almost abject horror, at the thought that I might be asked to stand up and propose the vote of thanks or make the speech at the next event.

Like so many people, my only previous experience of public speaking had been a four-minute talk at school and I remember so well the three weeks of suffering which preceded it. I had been conditioned to fear making a speech. I was convinced that I would make a fool of myself, possibly dry up, definitely would not be coherent and that I would be so nervous I would be unable to talk clearly. In fact, I would rather do almost anything than have to stand up and make a speech. So for years I didn't. I sat at many meetings and listened, on many occasions with the knowledge that I had ideas that could be of interest and which I should share — but I kept my mouth shut.

In 1965 I became so desperate with the income that we were getting from our farm and with the prices that were laid down by the government of the day that I decided that I could no longer sit back passively and take life as it was served up to me by others. I felt that, if we were to survive, something had to be done. There were countless other small farmers in dire financial straits at that time, so one day I called some 40 farmers together in Mayfield village car park and convinced them that we should take action against the government, beginning by blocking all the roads in Sussex on the forthcoming Easter Bank Holiday. My farming colleagues were persuaded. The roads in Sussex were indeed blocked on that Easter Bank Holiday and my speaking career had started.

I might add that I left the career of full time farming shortly after this, but this had little or nothing to do with the message that anybody can if they really want to.

Public speaking is really very easy and I am going to endeavour, through this book, to destroy the myths and legends that surround it. If you follow the ideas you will become a good communicator on your feet and will really enjoy the opportunity of communicating with many people rather than just individuals. Henry Ford said, 'Perhaps the greatest secret of business success is being aware of how results gravitate towards the person who can communicate his ideas persuasively.'

As the 1990s give way to the twentieth century, there is amazing communication technology available for all of us to use, yet never before has it been so crucial that people in positions of influence, power or management should be able to communicate through the spoken word effectively and persuasively in public.

If you want to be a great speaker, you can. You must start by asking yourself how important it really is to you. Let me emphasise once again, it is the most important skill that anybody with responsibility over others should master and, like all skills, it can be learnt.

The world that we live in is, and always will be, a people's world. In this book, I am going to show you the principles and methods of effective and persuasive communication. I will not be illustrating detailed, stereotyped speeches. The continual theme will be *'it is not what we say but how we say it'*.

Sell your speech

The foundation on which all effective speaking is built is accepting, believing and being convinced of the following statement:

> When people are on their feet speaking to an audience they should be doing one of two things and only one of two things; either entertaining or selling.

To clarify that statement, let me stress that the advice in this book is about live presentations and is not geared towards radio or television. In many cases, the methodology for radio and television can be the complete opposite to speaking to a live audience.

So let's go back to the statement that speaking in public is either an entertaining exercise or a selling exercise. Let's immediately clarify my understanding of entertaining, which can include the stand-up comedian or certain types of after-dinner speech. Therefore most opportunities for people to speak in public are opportunities for selling rather than entertaining and I am going to be so dogmatic as to say that, having removed the entertaining category, all speaking is or should be a selling process.

I am sure your initial reaction, like the vast majority of delegates who have attended my courses, is that the last statement is not only inaccurate but is also a bit over the top.

◀ ALL SPEAKING IS SELLING ▶

Let me ask you, what events or occasions are there when a speaker is communicating to an audience that they should not or would not be selling?

The first example that normally comes to mind is the teacher. I am sure all of us, if we think back to our school, college or university days, have sadly suffered the experience of listening to teachers or lecturers who had incredible knowledge about their subject, but while they were talking to us we became bored, uninterested, our attention wandered and possibly we did not even understand what on earth they were talking about.

Surely it is the duty of those communicators to transfer their knowledge to the minds of their listeners, so that the latter can either accept or even in some cases argue against the message that is being communicated. The transference of knowledge is most definitely a sales process. It is the duty of educators to gain acceptance of their message from their students and on acceptance a sales process has taken place.

Let's take another example. How about the preacher in

church? Surely this is not a sales process? It most certainly is. And how very sad it is that so few preachers have been trained to understand the importance of selling their beliefs. That is why many churches have difficulty filling two or three pews, whereas the world's greatest evangelist, Billy Graham, with in most cases the same beliefs and using the Bible as the foundation of his message, can fill a football stadium.

He is not necessarily a greater believer in his subject than the local preacher in the local church, but he has mastered the understanding of effective communication that enables his message to become so powerfully persuasive.

Let's have a look at some more examples.

How about the best man at a wedding? Yes, of course he is selling. He 'sells' the bridesmaids to the wedding guests — how beautiful they are with their attractive dresses on and so on. The bridegroom, on the other hand, has a go at selling his mother-in-law (some can be very convincing at this stage of their marriage). What does he do? He thanks her for all the work and preparation that went into the wedding.

One area of public speaking that I am sure we will instantly agree on is the barrister in court. As we know, this is most certainly a selling exercise as the barrister sets out to convince the jury about either the innocence or guilt of the defendant. One hopes that the judge, on the other hand, is completely impartial and his or her duty is to sell the law.

◀ *THE STIGMA OF SELLING* ▶

This chapter started off with a statement that it is imperative to grasp, assimilate and accept the importance of selling in public communication.

For many people there is a stigma attached to selling and sales-people. The prevailing view is that selling is not a nice career and salespeople tend to have unfortunate characteristics — they are pushy, they come out with funny expressions and they have all got their toes turned up from having them slammed in doorways. Thank goodness this stigma is rapidly diminishing as the profession of selling is becoming accepted as one of the most important professions, as nothing happens anywhere in the world until a sale takes place and salespeople bring in the money that everybody else can eventually live off.

For a minute, think of all the speeches and presentations you have sat and listened to. May I suggest that the ones you can instantly recall and remember with enjoyment or interest are those where the speakers were selling the subject they were speaking about rather than just speaking about the subject.

◀ A METHODOLOGY FOR ▶ SUCCESSFUL COMMUNICATION

What will unfold throughout this book is a methodology for successfully communicating your subject using persuasive skills that will get your listeners and audience to accept and enjoy what you have to say.

Why is it that some of the greatest speech makers in the land suffer from an enormous lack of credibility? You may have guessed that I'm talking about politicians. There are very few who communicate with credibility. There are even fewer who can inspire an audience and there are even fewer still who can motivate people and convincingly sell their ideas.

Yet if you consider all public speakers it is the politicians who commit some of the worst sins. Good public speaking should not be judged by the amount of time the speaker can keep going, or by the ability to speak with or without notes, or by the amount of speeches delivered in a year. Good public speakers should be judged by the response and reaction of their audience.

If I am giving the impression that I am condemning all politicians with these remarks, then let me correct that. There are, have been and always will be some brilliant orators, communicators and speechmakers in this segment of our society. Let me list just a few:

- Winston Churchill

- Enoch Powell

- Michael Foot

- Neil Kinnock

- Harold Macmillan

I am not going to promise that if you read this book and follow the guidelines you will become another Winston Churchill or Michael Foot — that is not the purpose of this book. The purpose is to enable the reader to become an effective, confident, enthusiastic and persuasive communicator, whether in dialogue or communicating to large numbers of people.

◀ *WHAT IS A SALESPERSON?* ▶

The simplest description of a salesperson is someone who helps people to make up their mind. And this is effectively achieved by making a logical case backed up with an emotional reason for making a decision.

It is commonly said that a good salesperson can sell anything. This isn't true — a good salesperson can only sell something he or she believes in. Perhaps that is why some of our politicians have difficulty.

Good, professional salespeople know they must be persuasive, but they can only be persuasive if they are really interested in the other person and gain sufficient information by asking the right questions.

Professional salespeople prepare their presentations well and talk about their clients' or customers' interests. Professional sellers illustrate their sales presentations with anecdotes and case examples to produce the 'I want' feeling. At the same time they communicate effectively and clearly the facts and features of a product or service. Finally they draw their presentations to a close by asking for the business.

As we go through the methodology of speaking for yourself, the similarity between selling and effective public speaking will become very clear. In the end let's be realistic, it is just good common sense.

This book is about the vast majority of us who, when we have an occasion to stand up and speak to an audience, will look forward to the occasion and possess the confidence that we can do it well and the knowledge that, when finished, our message will achieve the result that we are hoping for. But do remember, to be a successful communicator you must be persuasive.

P O C K E T   R E M I N D E R S

- A person speaking to an audience should only be either entertaining or selling
- All speakers are selling something ✓
- Good public speakers should be judged by the response and reaction of their audience
- A salesperson is someone who helps people to make up ✓ their mind
- The methodologies of selling and public speaking are based on common sense.

❝   W I S E   W O R D S   ❞

**If you want to cheer yourself up
cheer somebody else up.**

Bits & Pieces

2

Mastering Nervous Tension

The vast majority of readers of this book will fall into one of the following three categories:

- Those who have never spoken in public before

- Those who have — and it was a painful experience

- Those who enjoyed the experience and now want to do better.

I hope that there will be sufficient information in the book for everyone to find what they need. If you have never spoken in public before you may, like me, dread the thought of it and have perhaps kept your head below the parapet up to now to prevent the opportunity arising or the invitation being presented. Why? Almost certainly because of the fear of failure which, in turn, can lead to a subconscious fear of rejection and possibly the feeling that you are going to make a fool of yourself.

If you have had a bad experience of public speaking, you will almost certainly have experienced a crisis of confidence and even possibly, albeit dangerously, classified yourself as one not cut out for public speaking — the experience of failure leads to a lack of confidence which, in turn, can lead to a feeling of 'I'm no good at that'. You see, we are all conditioned by past experience. Every one of us is born with a positive outlook. But life's conditioning makes people negative.

Most of us were conditioned at a very early age to understand the meaning of the word 'no'. This was used on us by our parents almost certainly for what their own protective instincts told them were good reasons, eg 'No, don't do that' or 'No, you might hurt yourself'. The word 'no' was also used by our peers as a method of gaining control and eventually, as a result of this conditioning, 'no' prevented us from doing what we wanted and from achieving what we are truly capable of because we become conditioned to believe the negative. For some people the word 'no' can take on such a considerable importance in their subconscious mind that they feel rejected, doubt themselves or their ideas and believe that they are not capable.

What relevance does this have to public speaking? Very simply, in order to be an effective speaker you must first of all understand your own fears, dreads or excitements and then master your own nervous system to enable you as a speaker to give of your best.

◀ UNDERSTAND YOUR ▶ NERVOUSNESS

From my own simplistic point of view there are two types of nervousness that the public speaker should be aware of. The first occurs whenever we have to do something completely out of the ordinary for the very first time — the first sky-dive, the first ride on a horse. And the first time we stand up to speak in public. That nervousness can perhaps be described as a feeling of utter terror.

This feeling doesn't last and the more times you do what you are afraid of, the more the fear lessens. Remember that outstanding quotation:

The only way to conquer fear is to keep doing the thing you fear to do.

The second form of nervousness is extremely important and is the form of nervousness that the public speaker must master and harness.

I am sure you have seen or listened to an interview with a well-known actor. It is extremely common for the interviewer to say to the interviewee: 'You have been on the stage now for many years. Do you still suffer from stage fright or nerves?'

What do they say in reply? Invariably it would be something along these lines: 'Yes, and you know it never gets better.' And they may go on to describe their nervous tension. Some find they can't speak to their colleagues, others become irritable, some feel physically sick and others suffer from loose bodily functions!

Their experience is crucial for all public speakers to understand. First of all, let's accept that the people we see interviewed are the stars of their profession, not the also-rans. And these stars are sometimes in productions that can run for nine months or more, with a performance once a day or even twice. Yet they say that before every performance they experience nervous tension.

So what can we learn from them? This form of nervousness is a natural reaction. The actors are so intent on giving their best that the nervous system sets the adrenalin running and creates an uncomfortable feeling of nervous tension.

It can be summed up by saying they really care and they know that they are only as good as their last performance. Maybe without the nervous tension their performance would be lacking in depth, feeling, concentration and enthusiasm.

Adrenalin and nervous tension are essential parts of a good performance. Therefore you shouldn't worry about feeling nervous but quite the contrary — you should worry when you are not feeling nervous, because more than likely you will be about to give just another presentation.

◄ **DEALING WITH NERVOUS** ►
TENSION

Some people resort to alcohol in an attempt to master nervous tension. Let me state emphatically that in my view this is unforgivable. I would be very wary of allowing any speaker to address a gathering if the whiff of alcohol preceded his or her appearance.

Some people find that when they start speaking their hands shake, they feel as though their legs are trembling and their voice is quivering. There are, of course, genuine extreme cases — but the vast majority of speakers who think that this is happening to them do not realise that it is never noticed by an audience.

In the next few chapters we will be looking in more detail at ideas for developing confidence, building enthusiasm and creating the best possible environment for the mind and body to function together to deliver a good presentation.

The best technique I have discovered, after 20 years of speaking at conferences, conventions and seminars throughout the world (and, if I am honest with myself, I think my nervous tension is on the increase), is to take one or two deep breaths just before walking forward or standing up to give a presentation.

Be careful — unless you are extremely fit, more than one or two deep breaths could cause you to hyperventilate and knock yourself out. It would be extremely disconcerting for the event organiser to find the next speaker flat on the floor!

If it is possible, I have also found that taking some physical exercise a few minutes before speaking helps the adrenalin to flow and brings oxygen into the blood supply, which of course circulates through the brain. This could be a few press-ups or arm-swings.

This idea is also excellent for occasions when you are not experiencing any nervous tension and it is extremely important to get your adrenalin running.

So to master your nervous tension before and during the early stages of a public speech, a few deep breaths will steady the nerves. Holding your hands together or grasping the lectern will help if you are shaking. But above all else it is the planning and preparation of your presentation that will build your confidence and practice which will help you to overcome the tension.

Nervous tension is good as long as it is managed. It is a bit like stress. Stress is so good for us all as long as it is controlled.

Stress creates an element of pressure and helps people to raise the level of their thinking and performance. However, when stress is not managed or controlled through good time management, it can become a medical complaint and can be extremely dangerous. As with most things in life, the two extremes are to be avoided.

Never again fear the nervous tension. The time to be concerned is when there is none, as this is when a speaker can become so confident and care so little that the message being delivered will have no impact or feeling.

P O C K E T   R E M I N D E R S

- We are born positive — life makes us negative
- To be a good speaker you must understand your fear
- Nervousness can come from terror or `stage fright'
- The only way to conquer fear is to keep doing the thing you fear to do
- Adrenalin and nervous tension are essential parts of a good performance
- Deep breathing or exercise can help conquer the tension
- Nervous tension is like stress — good as long as it is managed.

❻   W I S E   W O R D S   **❾**

Fear defeats more people than any other thing in the world.

Ralph Waldo Emerson

3

Preparation

Confidence comes from thorough and accurate preparation. As we have already said, one of the biggest fears that most people have is the fear of speaking in public. This can of course easily be summed up as a lack of confidence.

In the next chapter we will be looking at methods of building confidence, but suffice to say for now that the most important stage of building confidence is covered in the following recommendation:

Research and prepare your talks well.

The more effort you put into the preparation, construction and writing of a talk, the greater will be the enthusiasm and enjoyment of your delivery.

Most speakers receive plenty of advance notice of a presentation that they are invited to deliver or an occasion when they are requested to speak. As soon as the event is confirmed, the preparation should begin.

So let's go through the stages in preparation most of which are in any case common sense.

◀ STAGE 1 — PREPARE A FILE ▶

Open a file or get a large envelope and write on the outside the details of the event and preferably, if you know it at this stage, the title of your talk.

◀ STAGE 2 — COLLECT IDEAS ▶

During the time leading up to the day when you actually write the speech, use the file or envelope to collate material that could be used. For example, you may be reading a newspaper and find facts and figures or even details of a thought process. Cut the article out and put it in your file.

Carry with you a blank pad and a pencil. Whenever you get an idea, capture it on your pad and put the note in your file. Keep the pad alongside your bed — many of us get good ideas when we are about to go off to sleep. Write them down and the following morning add them to your file.

Remember, we all get material from radio and television. Again, capture those thoughts and add them to your file. Maybe someone tells you a story or an anecdote which could be useful — write it down and add it to your file.

There are a great many speakers who keep a detailed filing system of material that they can call on for their various presentations. Make your speech writing easy — it obviously goes without saying that to sit down in front of a blank pad with no material to start from certainly makes the process extremely hard, in which case it is often put off until the last possible moment.

◄ *STAGE 3 — DECIDE WHAT* ► *YOU ARE AIMING FOR*

Before actually putting pen to paper to write your talk, you must first of all decide exactly what reaction you want to achieve at the end.

May I cast your mind back to Chapter 1 when I said emphatically that speaking in public is a selling exercise? It is only the frustratingly unprofessional also-rans of the sales world who will enter into a sales presentation without any idea of what they want to achieve at the end of their presentation.

If you don't know what you want, the audience won't know either.

So what sort of reactions could you be aiming for? Do you want your audience to:

- applaud
- make a decision
- take immediate action
- accept your message unanimously
- be hostile
- be bored
- be enthusiastic
- laugh
- cry?

Maybe you just want your audience to assimilate and understand your message.

Interestingly, you will find that having made a decision about what the purpose of your speech is, the actual writing and delivery of it become that much easier. Knowing the desired reaction, the action somehow becomes automatic. One of the basic philosophies of achievement is first to decide what you want, then the stages to get what you want are not really difficult. Remember the old cliché: *A person who is going nowhere normally gets there.*

◀ ## STAGE 4 — WRITE THE SPEECH ▶

Let's now look at the basic construction of all speeches. There should be:

- an opening
- a message
- a close.

We will consider in more detail in Chapter 4 what can go into the three segments, but we can first of all establish the principles.

Writing the speech

From your file or envelope of notes you have collected, list in any order all the thoughts, ideas and material that you have and that come to mind at this stage.

Secondly, from that completed list, select a sequence of items which follows a logical thought process. This will make it easier for you to deliver the speech and for your audience to understand it.

Thirdly, you can now, if it suits your personality, write the complete presentation as if you were going to read it, with paragraphs, sentences and punctuation.

Read your text and make the necessary adjustments until you are completely comfortable with its content, and possibly read it aloud or into a tape recorder. You can then move on into the fifth and final stage, which is to prepare the notes from which you will deliver your presentation.

◀ *STAGE 5 —* ▶
PREPARE YOUR NOTES

Remember that these notes are your speaking aid and must not be allowed to become a trap.

By now I am sure you will have gathered that this book is not endeavouring to teach you how to write and read the perfect speech. I am most certainly not qualified to be a great speech writer and my belief is that there are very few occasions when a speech should actually be read out. These few occasions occur within the realms of political and corporate diplomatic sensitivity, when the speaker has to be word perfect and a word taken out of context could have severe repercussions and conflict. In most circumstances, however, speeches should never be read out. Do remember that your audience can also read — you might just as well photocopy your speech and hand it out, then everybody can sit in silence reading the speech together. We have already said, and let me repeat again. *It is not what you say but how you say it.*

A few years ago I was listening to a public speaking trainer holding forth on a television programme that his audience should use a series of cards as speaking aids. My belief is that some people are comfortable with cards and others are not, and I am one of those that are not. I prefer to use a foolscap page with lines and a margin. You must discover what you are most comfortable with, but whatever it is you use, make sure you keep to the following principles. /

From your full written text, take the theme of a paragraph and make that a main heading. Then from the sentences jot down one or two words to remind you of the detail or the theme, so that your speaking aid ends up with just headings and sub-headings. You can use different coloured pens, you can under-line, you can 'box in' certain words and phrases, and you can use highlighting and asterisks. They all make your speaking aid more successful. Whether you are using a series of foolscap pages or cards, do make sure that each is numbered at the top.

DRYING UP

One of the biggest fears for an inexperienced speaker is the fear of 'drying up', or forgetting what to say.

There are two major causes of a speaker drying up. The first is having no notes because you believe you can speak 'off the cuff' or because you have memorised your speech. There are very few people in the world who have a sufficiently good memory and enough confidence to expose themselves to the risk of a memory lapse and speak without notes. I do not rec-ommend it and my best advice is never, under any circum-stances, speak without a speaking aid.

The second and perhaps by far the most common cause of the speaker drying up is that their speaking notes are not an aid but a trap. If you walk out in front of the audience with a tightly typed script or, even worse, a handwritten script in extremely small print, you might lose your place or your mind could go off at a tangent and depart from the script (there is nothing wrong in that — when you return to the script you won't be able to find what comes next). Many speakers think it is the done thing to speak without notes so they put their notes on a tiny piece of paper and can't actually read them.

Therefore in order to prevent the drying up syndrome it is essential that you make your handwritten notes in large writing. Do not use longhand but capital letters and make sure there is a good space between each line. You may find it helpful to underline your main theme in each paragraph with a coloured pen.

The acid test which will tell you whether your notes are going to be an aid or a trap is to stand three feet away from them and see if you can clearly read what you have written.

◄   *STAGE 6 — PRACTISE*   ►

The day before you are due to give your presentation, working from your speaking aid deliver the speech aloud either to a member of your family, a colleague or a tape recorder. The purpose of this is twofold:

*   to check the time length

*   to reinforce in your mind the sequence and the theme.

As far as the time length is concerned, you can be sure that the practice time will be totally different to the actual delivery because when you are speaking to your audience you may either talk more quickly or, on the other hand, more slowly. Experience will help you to be more accurate, but at least the practice run gives you a guide.

The final stage of preparation should be one more practise the night before your talk. This allows your subconscious mind to record the content overnight and will enable you to give a more confident delivery.

Before leaving the subject of preparation, let me ask you two questions:

- What is the purpose of your speech?
- Are you speaking for your benefit or your audience's?

As far as the second question is concerned, I am sure you will agree that it is always for the benefit of the audience. It is therefore your duty to make sure that you communicate effectively and accept that public speaking is not an ego trip.

You are not in front of your audience to demonstrate your memory or your communication skills. You are there to communicate a message with enough objectivity to achieve the reaction you have previously decided you want.

Do remember the old maxim:

Proper planning prevents particularly poor performance.

```
        P O C K E T   R E M I N D E R S

                        ✓
   ● Confidence comes from preparation
   ● The six stages of preparation:
       — Prepare a file
       — Collect ideas
       — Decide what you are aiming for
       — Write the speech
       — Prepare your notes
       — Practise
   ● Your are speaking for your audience's benefit.
```

❛ WISE WORDS ❜

Only the prepared speaker deserves to be confident.

Dale Carnegie

4

Content

We have already seen that the basic construction of all presentations is an opening, a message and a close. I am going to illustrate a number of examples of how to open a presentation, but first let me tell you a story.

There was a man who owned a donkey, but unfortunately it was untrained and had terribly bad habits. The man found he could do nothing with it. So he looked in the *Yellow Pages* and telephoned a donkey trainer. He explained his problem and asked about the cost of training, and they agreed that he should take his donkey to the donkey trainer's premises.

When he arrived, he once again explained his donkey's bad habits. The donkey trainer said he would start the training process immediately and the owner asked if he could stay on a while to watch and see what the trainer did. 'By all means,' replied the trainer. 'Hold on to your donkey.' He then walked across his yard into a shed and came out carrying a large wooden mallet, went straight up to the donkey and hit him with one sharp blow on his forehead. Naturally the owner was distressed and said, 'What on earth are you doing?' The trainer replied, 'The first stage of training is to attract his attention.'

It is the same when you speak to an audience — the first stage is to attract their attention.

◀ ## *TECHNIQUES FOR ATTRACTING ATTENTION* ▶

Let's describe a few ways in which this can be done.

TECHNIQUE 1 — MAKE A DESIRE-TYPE STATEMENT

In other words, say something that everybody wants to hear. This must of course be totally relevant to your presentation and to the audience.

For example: 'Ladies and gentlemen, during the next 30 minutes I want to discuss some ideas that could dramatically increase your income.'

Or: 'Ladies and gentlemen, during the next few minutes I would like to show you a formula that could considerably reduce your expenditure and save you a great deal of money over the next few months.'

Or: 'During the course of my talk, I hope to show you the exact stages in which you can manage, deal with and control the situation that now confronts you and that will enable you to turn it to your advantage.'

TECHNIQUE 2 — USE AN EXTRAORDINARY FACT ABOUT AN ORDINARY SUBJECT

This can be a great attention grabber. The *Guinness Book of Records* can be a fine source of irrelevant information which can nevertheless stimulate an audience to think.

TECHNIQUE 3 — USE VISUAL AIDS

You can produce an exhibit or, if you are using an overhead projector, a stimulating slide.

TECHNIQUE 4 — SET YOUR THEME

You could set the theme of your presentation by reading a text, a statement or a quotation.

TECHNIQUE 5 — TELL A HUMOROUS STORY

This method is very common and is certainly not the best, so I include it as a last resort.

If you are going to tell what can best be described as a joke at the beginning, definitely make it relevant to the gathering and, even better, personalise it with a name or two of people from the audience who will be known to everyone else But do make sure (and this is essential) that they would not be offended. More on that subject later.

◀ *CONSTRUCTING YOUR* ▶
PRESENTATION

The first few minutes of a speech are when the speaker is

normally most nervous. So it is essential for you to be very familiar with your first two or three minutes. This helps you to build confidence early and manage your nervous tension.

I am not going to go in any lengthy detail about the exact structure and content of any speech because it goes without saying that every presentation is different. So let's stick to the principles.

A speaker can make a brilliant speech from what could be described as 'poor content' if she or he has outstanding powers of delivery. But the reverse is not possible, which is why the majority of speeches are so boring.

To repeat what I said before: *It is not what you say but how you say it*. Here are a couple of formats that might make it easy for you to construct your presentation:

1. Present your facts
   Argue from them
   Appeal for action.

2. Show something that is wrong
   Show how to correct it
   Ask for cooperation.

◀ *EXPLAIN YOUR THEME* ▶

A rather annoying trend has developed where some speakers do not make it clear to their audience right from the beginning what the subject or the purpose of their presentation is. In other words, they are not focused and likewise the audience cannot be focused.

Imagine picking up a pair of binoculars and putting them to your eyes. The first thing you do is adjust them to get a clear image. You want to get the focus right. If for some reason you are unable to adjust the focus and obtain a clear vision, it becomes extremely uncomfortable and you put the binoculars down.

The above analogy illustrates the discomfort that an audience can feel if they are not sure exactly what is expected from them or what the speaker is talking about.

◄ *ONE MESSAGE AT A TIME* ►

Most speakers find that when they are writing or even delivering their presentation they have too much material and they are tending to cover too much subject matter.

Remember the parallel with selling. Salespeople can only sell one product at a time and it should be the same with a speaker — communicate one message at a time. It is utterly pointless to blast your audience with too much material which is the shotgun approach. Use a rifle instead. Shotgun pellets will cover a vast area when fired from about fifty yards. From about 120 yards they have a massive coverage but no penetration. Compare this with a .22 rifle: one bullet has massive penetration and can kill at a mile.

In summary and as a guideline, in a short talk of less than five minutes you should only attempt to cover one or a maximum of two main points. In a longer talk of, say, 30 minutes then try not to cover more than four or five ideas.

◀ ## PERSUADING PEOPLE TO LISTEN ▶

I have often been asked what I consider to be the most important tip for getting an audience to listen and to enjoy a speech. My reply is always that there are two essential recommendations: exploit the power of pictures, and relate the content to the audience.

USE PICTURE POWER

There is an old saying that '*People buy more with their eyes than they do with their ears.*' This is why in public speaking terms it is very effective to have some visual support. But if this is not possible, or not suitable, you can be even more effective by creating word pictures. I like to describe this as the speaker who uses 'picture power', getting the audience to see by using their imagination as well as hear.

Human beings are emotional creatures. Statistics show that a greater percentage of buying decisions are based on emotion rather than logic or reason. As a speaker with a duty to sell your beliefs or your ideas, it is essential for you to understand and use what could be described as emotional content and that can be done with word pictures.

Let's take a couple of examples. The first is a factual, logical attempt at talking to an audience about the subject of skiing.

EXAMPLE 1

For those of you who have not been skiing before, and if you should decide to go, the first stage would of course be to choose the resort and any travel agent will show you the brochures and give you advice according to how much you wish to spend. The next stage quite naturally will be to gather together some ski equipment. This can be purchased or hired. You would choose your ski suit and this could be a one-piece or a two-piece with an amazing selection of materials, colours and styles to choose from. You would need to choose your skis. These are normally governed by your physical height, although there is a tendency at some ski resorts for people to learn on shorter skis. Again there are different materials that these can be made from with varying flexibilities and breaking strengths. You would now need to choose your ski-sticks. You could have a straight ski-stick or one with a bend at the end and these are definitely governed by your physical height. Finally and most importantly of all comes the selection of the ski boot...

Now let's look at the same subject but including some picture power.

EXAMPLE 2

Having chosen the resort, arrived there and been equipped with clothing, skis, boots etc, it is natural to want to get on to the mountain as quickly as possible. This is often done by taking a cable car and this can be a wonderful experience in itself. As it silently moves up the mountain you see a magnificent sight left behind — the wooden timbered houses with their overhanging eaves. Your attention is then drawn to the majestic sight of the trees, pines and conifers that you seem to be going into. And then suddenly everything is obliterated from view as the cabin goes into the cloud and when it draws out you notice a completely new view with the tops of the mountains and the sun sparkling on the snow. The cable car

> comes to a halt. You get out and put on your skis and take
> the first movements. The sheer feeling of exhilaration, the
> crispness of the air and the sound of the skis on the snow.
> Marvellous!!

From these two examples I hope you can see the importance
of descriptive communication. What would be the purpose of
that speaker talking about skiing? If the intention was to raise
people's interest in the subject, he or she should have communicated clearly and (even though it may be offensive to you)
sold the subject of skiing. That can only be done by communicating effectively and selling the result.

If the introduction arouses the audience's interest they will be
even more interested in learning what is necessary in order to
go skiing. The speaker can then cover details of the skis,
clothes, boots, poles and the cost of various resorts.

What I am suggesting is the opposite of what most speakers do.
They spend a large part of their presentation rabbiting on about
the subject and then at the very end they get around to the
benefits or the object or the purpose or the result. Only at the
very end do they describe what it would be like if everybody
followed up or took action on what they have been talking
about.

I cannot stress strongly enough that when you are speaking
you talk about the result. Build a picture of the result. Sell the
result. Get your audience to want the result. The how, why,
what and when to achieve it then becomes acceptable and easy
to communicate and the audience will be interested.

You will have seen the very effective advertisements selling a
diet or a diet food — the effective advertisements show 'before
and after' pictures. Likewise companies that sell hair shampoo
show beautiful hair as the result, and companies that sell make-
up show beautifully made-up faces. They do not go into details
about how the product is made or how to use it.

RELATE THE CONTENT TO THE AUDIENCE

The second recommendation about holding the attention of an audience is to make sure that the content really does relate to the audience. You see, the error that some speakers make is that they talk either above or below their audience. They do not communicate *with* their audience. When you are selecting the content of what you want to communicate you must make sure that it relates to the majority of those listening to you.

One very simple test is to imagine yourself as a member of your audience and ask yourself the question — does this relate to me? Secondly — do I understand? If you are ever in doubt, lean towards a slightly more simplistic approach rather than the reverse. Your audience must be able to identify with what you are saying. Good speakers will identify with their audience at some stage, preferably early in their presentation, and this will be discussed in more detail later.

I am sure we all know that people's prime interest is in themselves, followed by their immediate family, their job, hobbies, etc.

TELL REAL-LIFE STORIES

There is a third recommendation for holding attention and also for maintaining a high level of interest in any audience, and that is to use real-life true stories, anecdotes and analogies. Whenever a speaker is telling a true story, the audience will be really interested.

To get your message across, enhance your content with a story or an experience. The late Norman Vincent Peale, one of the world's greatest communicators, was quoted in the quarterly *Journal of Speech* as saying that 'the true example is the finest method I know of to make an idea clear, interesting and persuasive.' An anecdote can develop the main points of a message.

When you are telling a true story, do wherever possible use the names of the people involved, so long as this does not cause any offence. If you are able to use people's names in your presentation you can be guaranteed maximum audience attention and you will have, as Dale Carnegie says, 'the priceless ingredient of human interest in your speech.'

COMMUNICATE WITH DIALOGUE

Some people are able to communicate through dialogue or conversation with another person. If you can do this naturally, it is a further excellent way of creating interest and holding attention.

◄ *ENDING THE PRESENTATION* ►

There are of course countless ways in which a presentation can be drawn to a conclusion. I am going to list a few, not in any order of importance, but purely as some possible ideas that may appeal to you for different occasions.

1. Summarise the main points. This should not be used in a short talk of less than six minutes as it would be far too repetitive. However it can be really effective for presentations where the content has to include a fair amount of detail in the content that needs to be re-emphasised and repeated.

2. Appeal for action: 'Let's get going.' 'Let's unite together'.

3. Pay your audience a sincere compliment. This should only be used when it is truly deserved otherwise it becomes insincere and it has become hackneyed and devalued in the

North American continent. But when appropriate it can be an excellent form of close and can provoke a warm reaction.

4. Raise a laugh by telling a joke or a story.

5. Use a quotation or a verse of poetry. Whatever you choose must always relate to the content and theme of the presentation. The same applies if you are using humour: it should always be part of the theme. There are certain occasions when a verse of poetry or a short, straightforward poem can reinforce a theme. Obviously if you were making a highly technical presentation to a group of directors in a boardroom, you would be unlikely to close with four verses of Wordsworth!

6. It is possible to build to a climax with good vocal technique. You might decide to become very loud or, on the other hand, very soft, or to speak very fast or very slow. You may have noticed that a lot of orators use a certain technique when they want a standing ovation: they repeat a theme three times in short sentences while raising the level of their voice, which causes the audience to break into thunderous applause or the desired standing ovation.

POCKET REMINDERS

- The basic construction of all presentations is:
  - opening
  - message
  - close
- First attract the audience's attention
- Be very familiar with your first two or three minutes
- Explain your theme
- Only one main point at a time ✓
- Use picture power
- Relate the content to the audience.

WISE WORDS

The greatest of all faults is to be conscious of none.

Thomas Carlyle

5

Holding Attention

I have been told that the maximum time an audience is able to maintain concentration is 20 minutes. Whether this is true or not I really don't know, but on that basis, throughout my speaking career, I have tried to take my audience off the subject every 12–15 minutes in order to prevent losing their attention. The techniques for relaxing concentration are some of those we have just been highlighting — namely tell a real-life story, use an anecdote or an analogy.

But the real secret of maintaining an audience's attention is to be enthusiastic.

◀   *ENTHUSIASM*   ▶

Let's return once again to the foundation of all effective speaking and that is that the speaker should be selling the subject about which they are speaking, speaking in public being a sales process. Have you ever been on the receiving end of a salesperson who is not genuinely enthusiastic about his or her subject? Please don't think about some of the artificial, creepy or smarmy salespeople that you have been faced with (there will always be a few) but bring to mind genuine salespeople who are genuinely enthusiastic about their subject.

Think of some of the great communicators on television, enthusiasts who have taken an otherwise intellectual subject and turned it into something of great interest and excellent viewing. Remember how David Bellamy made botany essential viewing on TV. *The Sky at Night* with the fascinating Patrick Moore is one of the longest running of all TV programmes. Sir David Attenborough has made his programmes on the natural world incredibly successful.

In another area, what is it that distinguishes one of the world's greatest management gurus, Tom Peters, from the thousands of others in the world of academia and business consultancy? Surely it must be the enthusiasm that he demonstrates in the delivery of his subject. This enthusiasm comes through on his TV and video appearances as well as his live speaking engagements.

All these personalities are enthusiastic about their subject. They are genuinely excited and they put their message across so well that I am sure we would all agree they believe in what they are saying. But so do the countless clerics in Britain who have great difficulty in filling more than two or three pews in their churches. Yes, they do tell stories and they have the greatest reference book in the world from which to draw their stories. The content of most of their sermons is excellent but the message is diminished and devalued because of the delivery. And sadly there are a number of other public speaking mistakes that are made which will be covered in later chapters.

Please do not get the impression that I am saying you have to be a raging extrovert in order to be an effective speaker. But most people find that they can be animated when they are talking about something that they truly believe in, and it is that animation which must be maintained in front of an audience.

So what is the difference? It is all very well to be animated in conversation when you are sitting in an armchair or across the table from a member of your family, a friend or a colleague, but it is a completely different situation when you are speaking to an audience. Nevertheless it is only a question of time before your confidence builds up and you can be just as animated in front of an audience.

Imagine placing a six-inch wide plank of wood on the ground. You would not have much difficulty in walking down that plank putting one foot in front of the other and keeping perfect balance and you would not be afraid of taking that walk. Now raise the plank 20 feet in the air, suspended on two tripods, one at each end. Your enthusiasm for taking the same walk would probably now have diminished. The walk would be exactly the same but the circumstances have changed.

Supposing you take a walk on the plank in the air with a safety net underneath and a couple of people on either side to help in case of an accident and you walk that plank from one end to the other without any mishap. May I suggest you would be able to turn round and do it again and after half a dozen or so walks you would be confident enough not to need human assistance and finally you would be happy to have the net removed.

So it is with being enthusiastic with your audience. The first time remember the lovely cliché: *Fake it till you make it.* By the third or fourth time the enthusiasm should come naturally.

Enthusiasm is *so* infectious. We are all naturally drawn towards people who exhibit this characteristic — someone you meet at a party or the child's bubbling enthusiasm returning home from school. We want to listen. We want to hear more. And in turn we can catch that enthusiasm.

◀ ## REMOVING NEGATIVE THOUGHTS ▶

If you do a lot of public speaking there will be times when, even though you are enthusiastic about your subject and about the opportunity to present it, before the presentation you experience something that removes your enthusiasm. It could be a crisis at home, a bereavement or even just a letter from the bank manager.

Remember the analogy of the actor. When you go to the theatre and pay a considerable amount for your ticket you do not expect to see the star of the show delivering a performance which is below par because he or she has received a letter from the bank manager or the family pet has just been rushed to the vet. In the same way all speakers have to put aside any worries or concerns and not share or burden their problems of life with their audience.

I am not sure what the exact percentage is but when a person tells others about their problems it is I believe only a person's very closest family and friends that care. The remaining 99 per cent either don't care or are glad.

So how do you remove that worry or pressure from your mind? You can do it very simply and very effectively. Most people completely undervalue the enormous capacity and capability of the human brain. We are all able to control what we think about. If you don't like a particular thought, remove it, take it out of your mind and tell yourself that you don't want to think it.

If you are a photographer, when you receive your prints and negatives back from the processor you discard those prints that are poorly focused or not up to standard. We are able to do exactly the same with our mind, so discard that worry or that negative thought.

◀ *REGAINING ATTENTION* ▶

Let's now suppose that for some extraordinary reason you have lost the attention of your audience and they are giving you the normal body language feedback — looking around the room, shuffling, most of the audience with arms folded leaning back in their chairs, continual glancing at watches, even drooping eyelids. It is essential for you to do something and in most cases you can't thump the table and say, 'Come on now, pay attention.' But you must do something.

I can illustrate this with a few examples of what — or what not — to do.

EXAMPLE 1

I once saw a speaker who had lost his audience's concentration. Seemingly by accident he suddenly moved his arm in a demonstrative gesture which connected with his flip-chart and easel. The whole thing crashed to the floor and some of the pens flew into the audience. Of course everyone woke up and there was a little light relief while the flip-chart was put back together. The speaker was then wise enough to wrap his subject up fairly quickly and he also slightly changed direction by telling a story and changing the level of his voice.

EXAMPLE 2

On another occasion a particularly boring speaker dropped all his notes on the floor. He bent down behind a rather large table to gather them up, disappearing out of sight, and the audience's reaction was 'Thank God he's gone'. Nevertheless, it did provide a break.

He rather sadly was so in love with his subject and so determined to deliver the whole of his text to his audience, regardless of whether they were interested or listening, that he immediately carried on where he had left off.

EXAMPLE 3

A few years ago I had a personal experience that on reflection could be used to 'get out of trouble' if you lose the attention of an audience.

The venue was a hotel in London and there were approximately 300 people in the audience. While I was speaking I smelt burning and noticed that the front row had also got a whiff of the same smell. It was very amusing to see first noses twitching, then people looking at each other, then at the ceiling at either side of the room and even a quick glance under the table.

So I said to the audience, 'I am sure I can smell burning. Has anybody else noticed?' There was an instantaneous response. The whole audience immediately breathed in with a look of genuine consternation. It happened that the chef in a nearby kitchen had in fact had a minor fire and on this occasion the hotel alarm did not go off and we did not have to leave the meeting room.

Now let's suppose that you had got the body language feedback that your audience was no longer listening. You could calmly announce to your audience, 'I am sure I smell burning, has anyone else noticed?' I will guarantee you a response — but there is a danger of losing your entire audience through the nearest exit!

What I am really saying is that if you have lost your audience's concentration, do something: change direction, raise or lower your voice, tell a story or just wrap up your talk.

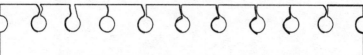

POCKET REMINDERS

- Keep your audience's attention by being enthusiastic
- Fake it till you make it
- Discard negative thoughts.

WISE WORDS

It's not what you say but how you say it.

Anon

6

Prepare yourself

People buy people first. So it says in all sales training manuals and courses. We all know and have been taught to make a good first impression and that people form an opinion within 30 seconds of a meeting. We all also know that in many cases the initial opinion we form changes at later meetings.

But from the public speaker's point of view it is essential to create a good first impression which helps to build credibility and respect in the minds of the audience. And that first impression as the speaker stands up or walks out in front of the audience will be created by his or her visual appearance.

◀ *PHYSICAL APPEARANCE* ▶

Let's consider a few details that can help to build the respect and credibility you are looking for.

The clothes that you wear must be smart. I personally believe that all male speakers should wear a suit and the jacket of that suit should remain buttoned. I do accept that some speakers giving a long presentation like to start wearing their jacket and then remove it — sometimes this is acceptable in a very informal seminar or similar occasion. In most cases it is preferable for speakers to remain professionally dressed. Some managing directors and chairmen intentionally remove their jacket when communicating with their own people. I find this to be an acceptable attempt to remove a 'them and us' feeling and create greater identification, but it should only be used by very senior people.

Minor details should not be forgotten because they can cause distraction. For example, a tie that is out of place can mean that the audience is thinking 'Why is that tie out of place? Why didn't the speaker check it in the mirror?' They might even construct an imaginary scenario about a speaker who avoids mirrors because of a bad experience at some stage. The result is an audience who are not listening to the speaker but thinking about his appearance.

Your hair should be properly groomed, shoes smart and jewellery should be limited.

Confidence, as we have already said, comes from thorough and accurate preparation, but it can equally be built by having a good outward appearance. If speakers feel that they look good, their mental preparation and their confidence in their delivery will be enhanced.

One of the first outward signs that people are going through a tough period in their personal lives is that they let the standard of their appearance fall. Their hair is less likely to be groomed, their clothes are not pressed or laundered as regularly and they start to look shabby or frayed at the edges.

Have you ever worried about arriving at an evening event

where all the guests are dressed in dinner jackets and long evening dresses and you are in a lounge suit or a day dress? In that situation you would not be confident. You are the same person, but your clothes have reduced your confidence.

It is the same for a public speaker — the smarter the appearance, the greater the self-confidence.

◀ 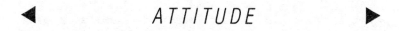 *ATTITUDE* ▶

As well as being conscious of your external appearance, you must also make sure that you are going to speak with the right attitude. And that attitude is of course positive rather than negative.

So many speakers seem to hold a negative self-image just before a presentation. They say to friends and colleagues or even more dangerously they think things like, 'I'm not looking forward to this,' 'I hate public speaking,' 'I am just not a good public speaker,' 'I just didn't have enough time to prepare my speech well' and so on and so on.

These are all negative statements, negative thought processes. And they all make it much harder for a speaker to give a good presentation.

Instead you must think positively. Now I am not saying that you have to go around saying to people 'I am a great speaker' or 'I am really looking forward to this,' but you definitely must and should be saying it to yourself.

What the mind of man is able to conceive and believe it is forced to achieve.

We still underestimate the incredible power of our brain and, even more importantly, our subconscious. *Whatever we fear in life invariably happens.* So it is essential to fill your mind not with fears and negative thoughts but with positive thinking and images of success.

I remember seeing an interview with the outstanding British athlete David Hemery. He was recalling that on his second appearance at the Olympics he mentally prepared himself for losing the title. He felt he had to come to terms with not winning, just in case he didn't. He was so uncertain about whether he would be able to cope with not winning that he spent a great deal of time mentally preparing himself for this happening.

I'm sure you can guess the result — he did not win. And he said that his mental attitude was the main contributing factor to his not breaking the tape.

Mentally prepare yourself by saying, 'I am a good speaker,' 'My audience is going to enjoy this presentation.' Visualise your audience enjoying being involved and enthusiastically applauding at the end. See your audience as really nice people.

Say to yourself continually, 'It's going to be good, it's going to be great, it's going to be good.'

◀ *FINAL PREPARATIONS* ▶

The final stage of your preparation is always to arrive at the venue with plenty of time to spare, giving yourself a chance to get the feel of the room, hall or auditorium. This will also give you the opportunity to check the table arrangements, lighting, microphones, lectern position and so on. We will cover this in more detail in Chapter 11.

You will need to know where you will be sitting before your

presentation and which way you will have to walk. If you are speaking on a platform, check to make sure that the steps are in place so that you don't trip and fall flat on your face. That would certainly reduce your confidence!

If you are using visual aids, it is of course essential to check that the machines are in place and working properly. If you are using slides, it is always advisable to have a rehearsal.

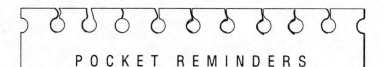

POCKET REMINDERS

- The first impression is important ✓
- Confidence comes from knowing you look smart
- Develop a positive attitude
- Arrive early and check out the venue.

' WISE WORDS **'**

The music that can deepest reach, and cure all ill, is cordial speech.

Ralph Waldo Emerson

Delivery

The speaker walks onto the platform or stands up to commence to speak. What should happen first?

◀ ## BEFORE YOU SPEAK ▶

Before the speaker actually starts the verbal communication, he or she must gain the audience's acceptance. The first few seconds will have a significant effect on the eventual outcome.

So what do professional speakers do? They pause and cast an eye over the audience with a gentle smile.

Let us analyse this in detail. What is the normal relationship between audience and presenter? In most cases the audience is sitting and waiting, the speaker is introduced, the audience thinks, 'Is this going to be of interest?', 'Am I going to be bored?', 'I wonder how good a speaker this is?', and possibly even, 'I wonder how long this is going to take?'

You see these are all barriers and it is the duty of the speaker to break them down. The speaker who starts off as we have just described above commences the process of 'barrier removal'.

Let me remind you once again that speaking is selling and of the cliché: *People buy people first.* It is the duty of speakers, as it is in the sales world, to sell themselves first.

Smiling starts to develop a relationship with the audience, relaxes them and may even generate a smile in return. There is a Chinese proverb that says: *He who cannot smile ought not to keep a shop.*

◀ ## A SPEECH OR A CONVERSATION? ▶

The speech or presentation now commences and you are embarking on what is called 'public speaking', a frightening phrase. Because of our conditioning, it has the wrong connotations.

Someone who sets out to give a public speech is going to deliver the material come what may, regardless of the audience's reaction or feelings. He or she is going to unload the speech on the audience. I prefer the phrase 'a public conversation'. We are familiar with conversation as a two-way process, which is what public speaking should be. The speaker delivers the speech but the audience gives feedback through body language.

In a normal conversation between two people, one person says something, the other replies and the first responds according to that reply. I might add that not all conversations go like this, as some people never listen to what the other is saying! Similarly a good speaker must be able to adjust the prepared text according to the audience feedback. Body language will be discussed in more detail a little later.

What I am saying is that you as a communicator must visualise yourself having a conversation with your audience, even though it is only you who is doing the speaking.

◀ *EYE CONTACT* ▶

As part of the technique of having a conversation with a group of people, eye contact is crucial to help make it easy for your audience to listen to you.

No one likes meeting and talking to a person who is unable to look you in the eye, who perhaps looks over your shoulder, at the ground or out of the window. That individual is normally treated with an element of suspicion or possibly even a feeling of mistrust. Yet it is quite extraordinary how many speakers in public situations have great difficulty in maintaining eye contact.

You must consciously make sure that you are continually looking into the eyes of your listeners. However large your audience and even if you are speaking from a platform that is well lit and your audience is in the dark, you must always be scanning your audience.

> I once sat through an hour-long presentation by the managing director of a small engineering company. He walked to the front and wrote three words on the blackboard: 'Welcome, good morning'. He spent the next hour continually glancing at the blackboard which, in turn, caused the audience to look at the blackboard and wonder what he could see that they couldn't.

As a general tip, it is much easier to speak to people who are smiling than it is to people that are glaring at you. So if it should ever happen you are particularly nervous about a particular occasion, plant a 'smiler' in the audience. He or she will be a good focal point and will give you moral encouragement — but please resist the temptation to address your whole presentation to that person. Keep your eyes moving and every so often 'recharge' yourself from the smiler.

While on the subject of eye contact, it is a common mistake for a speaker to make too much eye contact with the VIPs in an audience. Do fight the temptation to look in their direction too regularly.

◀ SPEAKING POSITION ▶

What is the best position to adopt while presenting? My own view is that all speakers should present on their feet. Whenever a speaker stands up it increases the value and importance of what she or he has to say.

When you have finished and want to develop a question session or discussion, it is then acceptable and extremely effective to change to a sitting position. Sitting down implies informality and makes question sessions and discussions more likely to develop. But please always stand up to make your presentation.

There are a number of aspects relating to stance that are important.

PACING

Some people develop, through nervous tension, a habit of pacing and can pace up and down the length of a platform. This can be a terrible distraction for the audience as their eyes follow the speaker from one side to another. It is a little like watching two tennis players in action, but with one performer the rocking motion can eventually cause the audience to drift into a relaxed state of sleepiness.

I might add that the pacer makes a great deal of eye contact, but with the floor, although there may be a glance in the direction of the audience from time to time just to make sure they are still there.

Obviously movement is good but as a guideline it should only be one pace from your central speaking point. Therefore, if you may be using a flip-chart, overhead projector or any other presentational aid, try always to position this one pace from your central speaking point.

TABLE OR LECTERN

Some speakers like to make their presentations from behind a table, others prefer to work from a lectern. As far as a table is concerned, it does provide the speaker with a feeling of security but also creates a barrier between the speaker and the audience. Tables and lecterns have only one purpose, as a place on which to rest your notes since it goes without saying that you should never be holding your notes. And while on that subject you will no doubt have seen speakers who waggle their notes at the audience or had occasions when you have attempted to count the pages of notes to see how long the speech is going to last.

As a good guideline, always opt for a small lectern and try never to speak from behind a table. If there is no lectern available, select the smallest possible table and preferably speak from one side of it rather than from behind.

If you have never used a lectern before, practise. Lecterns are not there to be leant on as you will appear to be preaching, which is acceptable in the pulpit but not in normal presentations.

It is perfectly acceptable to be behind a lectern for the first few minutes and then gradually to move away from it as your speech progresses.

POSTURE

Distracting postures include:

- carrying all your weight on one leg

- having one shoulder pointed to the audience, which makes you appear introverted

- continually backing away.

The right posture is facing straight towards the audience.

◄ *BODY LANGUAGE* ►

Body language on the part of both speaker and audience is now accepted as a significant method of communication, so it is essential for professional communicators to understand their own body language and be able to read the information being communicated by their audience.

HAND MOVEMENTS

Some speakers, particularly at the beginning of their speaking career, find that nervousness causes them to develop two uncontrollable objects at the end of their arms — their hands. Sometimes they are folded behind the speaker's back, sometimes they are folded in front, sometimes they go into trouser pockets and sometimes they play with coins or keys. It has been known for speakers to put a hand on their hip, or to pick their nose, pull an ear lobe, or even scratch their backside.

Some people nervously fiddle with a ring and others hold on to a spring-loaded ball-point pen that can make a distracting clicking sound: inaudible to the speaker but it can drive an audience potty.

These are all major distractions that a speaker can be in control of. Hands should be seen and always be in front of the body. Good hand movements can complement and enhance the value of what is spoken. Speakers who synchronise their hand movements with their words will communicate more effectively.

Let's look at some of the dos and don'ts of hand movement. The hands should always be kept open, although from time to time a clenched fist can be used to emphasise a point of strength. Hands with fingers kept open signify a more open type of person.

The palms of your hands should not be pushed at an audience with fingers upwards as this implies rejection, so you should always attempt to keep the back of your hands towards the audience. Showing your palms to the audience with your fingers pointing towards the floor is more acceptable as it implies help me, support me.

A pointed finger wagging at an audience implies that you are talking down to them. Parents wag a pointed finger at their children or their household pets and this is normally an admonishment.

An occasional circle movement with your arm can be very effective when combined with a phrase like, 'Let's get started', 'lets agree on this point' or even 'let's complete the contract now'. It draws the audience closer to you and creates an environment of agreement and pulling together in the same direction.

Hand movements must be natural and I do accept that many people have difficulty in communicating or gesticulating with their hands. So if it is too unnatural for you, just keep your hands together in front of you. If it is comfortable for you it will be comfortable for your audience.

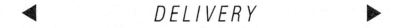

DELIVERY

Now let's discuss the actual delivery of the words. I want to re-emphasise that *It's not what you say but how you say it.*

The importance of enthusiasm and personal excitement has already been discussed. It is of course your facial expression and body language as well as your voice that convey the enthusiasm.

We have all suffered the experience of listening to a speaker with brilliant content but a boring delivery which could not sustain the message.

Examples include speakers who speak in a monotone or only at one speed. So vary your voice, sometimes be loud and sometimes be soft, put emphasis on certain words and phrases. Sometimes speak faster and then again slower. It is your voice and the emphasis that you place on certain words that can bring your prepared text alive.

SILENCE

One of the most powerful techniques that can be used in conversation as well as public speaking is the use of silence.

If you have a very important point that you want to get across to your audience, pause for a second or two before stating your message and then, even more importantly, allow a few seconds of silence immediately after. The silence before generates a feeling of expectation. The silence after allows time for your message to be assimilated and thought about.

Sadly many speakers devalue what may be an outstanding quotation or a strong message by not allowing sufficient pauses, silence or thinking time to let the audience take in the power of what they have just said.

We have all heard interviews with great comedians. They regularly praise their personal heroes by referring to their timing. What do they mean by timing? It is surely the pause before the phrase. The pause after allowing the message, the story, the joke or the anecdote to be assimilated by the audience.

Some comedians find it comes naturally to them. Others have to learn and it is the same with public speaking. It comes from practice and from experience but, more than anything else, it comes from a willingness and determination to strive for perfection in your public communication. When you are developing your speaking ability, if you are fully concentrating it is easy to judge the reaction you get from your audiences and at the end of each presentation think back to points where you got the reaction that you hoped for and where you got an unexpected reaction. But every time the reaction has to be earned and does not come as a right because you use the same words.

ENTHUSIASM

If you are reading this book because you are about to attempt your first speech, you may think that all this sounds too difficult. Let me assure you that timing does come with practice, but don't worry too much about it. It is much more important to be enthusiastic and to be positive.

You will never lose if you combine sincerity with enthusiasm, as long as it is genuine. And you can maintain and build a positive attitude of mind by always looking for the good and expecting the best.

We live in a world where we are fed a daily dose by the radio, television and newspapers of misery, strife, hunger and warfare from around the world. Most of this we can do very little about. Whatever the economic climate is, expansion or recession, there will always be people who say it's going to get worse. So look for the good, concentrate on positive achievements, look to the future with hope and always convey to your audience a feeling of hope.

With the development of natural enthusiasm, you will become a great presenter. There are many outstanding speakers with little or no education, slightly inarticulate but with tremendous enthusiasm who are sought out by organisations throughout the world.

POCKET REMINDERS

- First gain the audience's acceptance ✓
- A smile start to remove the barriers
- Public conversation rather than public speaking
- Maintain eye contact
- Make your presentation standing up
- Face the audience
- Synchronise your hand movements with your words
- Use silence
- Develop natural enthusiasm ✓
- Make sure the audience know how long you are speaking.

WISE WORDS

The greatest discovery of my generation is that human beings can alter their lives by altering their attitudes of mind.

William James

8

Avoiding bad habits

Let's look at some of the bad habits that will not only switch your audience off but can also bore them, have them looking at their watches or even counting light bulbs in the ceiling.

◀   *SELF-IMPORTANCE*   ▶

One very effective method of losing audience identification is to build your own importance. For example, a speaker may say something like:

> Ladies and gentlemen, the point I now wish to tell you is something on which I have now been recognised as the world authority. I have had 20 years' experience and made numerous appearances on radio and TV and books and articles have been written about my experiences.

I do accept that the example may itself overstate the case, but there are nonetheless many speakers who attempt to build up their own importance to try to justify a theme or a message that they want to bring to their audience — all they do is switch the audience off.

In Chapter 11 I will explain how an introduction by somebody else can prevent the speaker falling into this ego trap.

APOLOGISING

The second habit to avoid is beginning your speech with an apology. Everybody has heard the classic phrase 'unaccustomed as I am . . .', but apologies come in many different forms:

- I'm sorry I'm late

- I'm sorry I'm unprepared

- I have nothing very important to say

- I am sorry to take up your time.

Apologising immediately devalues both the speaker and the presentation. If an apology in any form is due to an audience it is best done by the person introducing the speaker.

SMOKING AND ALCOHOL

Smoking while speaking is unforgivable, extremely rude and should never happen.

I have mentioned alcohol earlier and it is advisable never to take alcohol before speaking. Having said that, I recall a situation a few years ago when I was suffering from a slipped disc. I attended various doctors for treatment and went to chiropractors and physiotherapists. I visited an osteopath and tried faith healing and acupuncture, all to no avail. The only solution was to have a laminectomy. But before the date set for the operation I still had three or four speaking engagements to complete. My back was now causing me so much pain it was virtually impossible for me to stand upright. Painkillers were not strong enough and my doctor advised me to use alcohol. I arranged for my eldest son, Lyster, to drive me to the events and 20 minutes before speaking I drank about a quarter of a bottle of whisky. This deadened the pain and I was able to speak for about an hour and a half without ever once slurring my words.

◀ *FACTS AND FIGURES* ▶

The fourth habit to avoid is relating streams of facts and figures to an audience. They will not be remembered so the exercise is pointless. Now I do accept that many presentations depend on the imparting from the speaker of facts and figures to support their message. If that is the case, the facts and figures must be in visual form either on a slide, overhead projector transparency, a flip-chart or in the form of a handout.

Visual aids will be covered in Chapter 12. As far as handouts are concerned, only give a handout to the audience when you want them to read it. I have seen many potentially good presentations ruined by speakers distributing handouts, in some cases even the complete text of the speech, before their presentation. If we are given something to read, the temptation is too strong to do anything other than read it, however good the speaker may be.

I was once invited to a conference about print and printing materials. The conference started at 8.30 in the morning and between 5.00 and 5.30 there was a presentation from the international sales director. One of his themes was the impact of good colour photography. As he concluded his speech he handed the all-male audience a bundle of magazines that he had just brought back from Amsterdam.

The next speaker was the finance director who was due to speak until the conference ended at 6.00. The magazines were being passed round the audience but there were not enough to go round — I am sure you can guess the result. The poor finance director had no chance whatsoever of holding his audience.

Incidentally, the organisers of the programme were completely at fault in putting that sort of presentation at the end of a hard day's concentration by the delegates.

◀ *JARGON* ▶

Fifthly, avoid flowery words, in-company jargon or terminology that your audience may not be familiar with. At the same time you must be realistic. If terminology and abbreviations are expected and are the norm, then it is correct for the speaker to communicate at the same level as his or her audience.

However some speakers, who see public speaking as an ego trip, search for words or phrases that are not used on a day-to-day basis but they feel that it is an important part of public speaking to demonstrate their command of the language.

◀ *TALKING DOWN* ▶

The sixth habit to avoid is what I call the 'harmless talk-down'.

There are many instances, a slip of the tongue or even crass stupidity, that can ruin a presentation.

A well-respected guest was invited to make a speech at a bankers' dinner in Manchester. There was a mixed audience and the guest speaker began as follows: 'Ladies and gentlemen, I want to thank you for inviting me to speak as your guest here tonight, but I had no idea that this was going to be a mixed audience so I have adjusted my speech accordingly!'

What a disaster that presentation turned out to be! If he had only thought of putting himself in his audience's shoes he would have understood the reaction. The women felt, 'Oh, what a shame — he's left all the best bits out'. The men were embarrassed that the women would feel that they shouldn't have been there and that what was said was a direct put-down to the women present. The speaker met with very little warmth or positive body language and would certainly not be invited again. He made no sale that night.

◀ *JOKES* ▶

Many people feel that humour is important in a presentation, but let's be realistic — some people have the ability to tell a joke or imitate an accent or be a good raconteur, and others do not. If you are not confident of your joke-telling ability, leave it out. Remember the phrase: *If in doubt, leave it out.*

Some of the best humour is not the set-piece joke. It is the statement or phrase that the audience twists to a different connotation. They may be appearing to laugh at you, but they are not. They are really laughing with you. And if people are laughing, they are buying.

Now let's suppose you did tell a joke or story and you didn't get a big laugh or the reaction that you were hoping for, but instead a polite, embarrassed giggle. There is a little technique that you can use that may get you out of trouble:

> Mr Aspen [the chairman, respected and known to all the audience] told me that story three weeks ago. I thought it was lousy and I did say you wouldn't laugh — you've all just proved me right.

You will normally get a laugh, even if only a tension-relieving laugh, and Mr Aspen will clearly enjoy the twist as well. He would certainly not be offended as long as you are not breaking our next rule.

 ## DIRTY JOKES

Dirty jokes are definitely taboo. Don't tell them. They are one of the main causes of audience embarrassment and loss of acceptability for speakers. To make the point, I want to high-light a simple example.

EXAMPLE

Imagine you have been invited to be the speaker at the Rugby Club Annual Dinner. Now you might consider that this is definitely one occasion when it is your duty to research and deliver one or two really dirty jokes. But let's suppose that one stalwart member of the club is known to his colleagues to be extremely offended by unsavoury jokes. You unknowingly launch into your presentation and deliver your prepared jokes. How will your audience respond? May I suggest they will show embarrassment and empathy for the person who will have been offended. And you will have lost your audience.

I am not being prudish. The right joke in the right company in the right place can be extremely funny. But again, if you are uncertain then leave it out.

 ## SNIDE COMMENTS

Making snide comments about a religion, a race or a political party is not so much a bad habit as a bad mistake because it normally only ever happens once to a speaker. If there is even one person in an audience that can be offended by a speaker's snide or unnecessary remarks, that speaker will lose empathy and audience identification.

> A great friend of mine who is an excellent speaker faced this problem on one occasion when he told a very amusing and philosophical Jewish story. As there were two people present who were Jewish and they were known to others in the audience, he lost his audience empathy. In fact, in this instance he did not offend the two Jewish members — as we all know they have an incredible sense of humour and most of their humour is based on themselves.
>
> But my friend could have prevented the loss of his audience by beginning with, 'Let me tell you a story told to me by my good friend Sharon Levi. . .'

PUT-DOWNS

Peoples' minds must be regarded as receivers. A receiver that is not switched on or tuned to the right wavelength is of little use. Using this analogy, having switched your audience on you must keep them tuned to your wavelength. Talking down to them can instantly persuade them to change channels. For example:

- 'Ladies and gentlemen, I am sure you don't know...'
- 'I expect you are not aware...'
- 'You probably have never experienced...'
- 'You probably don't know what I'm talking about...'

In each of these examples, the speaker normally then goes on to tell the audience what they didn't know, haven't experienced or weren't aware of. But what should that speaker do to keep the audience tuned in?

It is really very simple: *build your audience up. Don't put them down.* Give them credit for knowledge or experience they might otherwise not have had. Why not say:

- 'I expect you know ...'
- 'I am sure you are aware of ...'
- 'You have probably experienced ...'

and then go on to give the message that needs to be communicated.

 # PUBLIC CRITICISM

The final bad habit to avoid relates more to a manager speaking to their own internal members of staff. But public criticism can again cause loss of empathy, identification and at worst entirely the wrong result.

Let me take your mind back to the beginning of this book where I recommended that you decide the reaction you want before writing your talk. You maybe in a situation where part of your presentation has to be devoted to correcting either bad performance or bad business behaviour, so you have to give a dressing-down to your people in public.

The first point to make is obviously that criticism must of course relate to a number of people and definitely never only to one person. Individual criticism, as all managers know, must always be given privately.

EXAMPLE

A manager addresses his team at their monthly meeting:

> Ladies and gentlemen, as you are well aware our sales figures are abysmal and it is obvious that this is due to your lackadaisical approach. Your calling rate is atrocious, your paperwork is even worse and you probably spend half the day asleep in some lay-by.

In that example the manager is making a direct attack. Although the points being made may be justified, the comments and opinion will be received with hostility and will not necessarily achieve the desired reaction. To achieve a positive reaction, motivational communication has to be used. And a better way of getting the same message across to a group of people would be through the third-party attack. How about the following as an alternative:

Ladies and gentlemen, as you know our sales figures are not up to our normal standard. I know you all want to regain the strength that we previously had. There are many organisations in the current market-place whose salespeople are showing a lackadaisical approach, whose calling rate is atrocious and whose paperwork is even worse. And I bet they spend a great deal of their time asleep in some lay-by.

Let us look at how we can direct our performance towards our targets and goals.

The second format will draw that team of people together. The manager will get the reaction that is hoped for.

So whenever you as a manager have something really *important* to say, you can be ten times stronger when making a third person attack rather than a direct attack.

P O C K E T   R E M I N D E R S

- Don't exaggerate your own importance
- Don't begin with an apology
- Don't smoke or drink alcohol
- Don't bombard the audience with facts and figures
- Avoid irrelevant jargon
- Put yourself in your audience's shoes
- If in doubt, leave it out
- Don't offend your audience
- Keep the audience on your wavelength
- Use the third-party approach to criticism.

WISE WORDS

I hate fear so I eliminate needless risks.

Jackie Stewart

9

Developing good habits

You will recall one of our central themes, that public speaking is a sales process.

◀   *PERSONAL PRONOUNS*   ▶

The first good habit is careful use of the crucial words 'I', 'we', 'you' and 'they'.

The word 'I' should be used sparingly. It is best used when referring to your own past experience or mistakes. It is better not to use it in the context of building your own importance or how clever or smart you may have been.

The greatest speakers use 'I' very rarely and normally to help develop audience identification. What do I mean by audience identification? I mean finding and sharing some common ground with your audience. This can be either experience or common interest, but it is extremely important in developing not only identification but empathy.

The words 'we' and 'us' are 'good news' words and they communicate extremely well, so whenever you have good news to impart, use 'we', 'us', 'you' and 'your'. On the other hand, when you have bad news, you are being critical or cynical or in any way negative, even if you are talking about a negative future trend, try always to use the word 'they'.

Many managers talk at company conferences and address the audience as 'you' rather than 'we'. This creates an unnecessary division and does not motivate people to respond in united cooperation. Management communication skills in so many cases are very poor, which has developed mistrust and lack of loyalty. Take the manager who stands in front of his people exalting them to greater performance and using phrases such as, 'I want you to strive harder during the next 12 months, you will all have to work harder to keep your jobs.' How much better the reception would be if he changed the 'you' to 'we'. On the other hand, when a manager is thanking his or her people for some achievement and the recognition should be heaped on the audience, she should be saying, 'Ladies and gentlemen, during the past few months your achievements have been outstanding. You have reached your targets and may I thank you for your tremendous performance.'

◀ *EMPATHY* ▶

Our second good habit is understanding the importance of audience empathy. In other words, putting yourselves in their position and seeing from their point of view.

For example, if you are a man, never allow yourself to use the phrase 'the wife'. It will instantly switch off the women in the audience and is a direct put-down to your partner. Instead you should say 'my wife' followed by her first name. This gives a feeling of respect and creates audience empathy.

◀ ## THE WORD 'TRUE' ▶

When you are telling a true story do use the word 'true', but don't ever devalue it by prefacing an untrue story with the word 'true'. It's a fabulous word and when used correctly in telling real-life anecdotes you will always hold your audience's attention.

◀ ## KEEPING TO TIME ▶

The fourth good habit is being totally professional in sticking to your allotted time. Many presentations have a printed programme with times for each session and your audience expects you to speak for the time given in the programme. Some conference organisers do not allow sufficient comfort breaks and members of the audience will wait until the end of a session before rushing to the loo. That's the first very important reason to stick to your time.

The second reason is courtesy to the speaker who may be following you. It is extremely rude to carry on speaking into somebody else's allotted time. Thirdly perhaps the most important reason for sticking to your time is that if an audience knows you are due to be finishing at a certain time and you are still speaking, they will not be listening. They will more than likely be wondering how long you are going to go on for. And worse, if you should ever be speaking into a lunch, coffee or evening meal break, your audience is guaranteed not to be listening. So all your words are wasted words.

It is far better to leave some of the content out if necessary. Nobody will know what they have missed. It is certainly preferable to finish too early than to overrun. Remember the principle: *When you have nothing else to say, stop.*

Suppose you had been asked to speak for 30 minutes and a glance at your watch told you that at 23 minutes you were about to finish your prepared text. Do not attempt to keep going. It will become repetitious and, if you adopt the sales principle, you will talk yourself out of your sale.

> When you start your presentation, your audience traffic lights are at red. Through your presentation, you build their interest and desire and the light turns to amber. You draw your presentation to a close and the green light is now showing. Now if you keep talking, it is very easy to switch the audience straight back to red.

◀ ACCENTS ▶

The fifth point is not so much a good habit but more developing understanding. One of the myths of public speaking, and rather tragically many public speaking trainers seem to concentrate on, is that accents have to be trained out and enunciation has to be worked on. Trying to train out an accent is totally unnecessary.

If you decide, either through their own wishes or business necessity, that you are going to speak in public, you must maintain your own personality which, of course, includes your accent or dialect. If you try and train your accent out or change it, you will end up appearing artificial.

So long as a speaker can be basically understood, his or her sincerity, belief in the subject and most importantly enthusiasm will always carry the day. I have known many potential speakers who have been conscious of their dialect or accent and that made them afraid of making presentations.

I accept that the BBC quite rightly trains its personnel in enunciation, but that is for a completely different situation. Many of the techniques that have to be used on radio or TV are the complete opposite of those that would be used in front of a live audience.

I have had people come to me for help and training with what they considered a speech defect in the form of a stutter. If you have friends with a stutter, tell them never to worry. They will get tremendous empathy from their audience and the audience will always listen. Speakers who stutter are almost guaranteed to sell their concept to an audience.

I have found that while speaking abroad in my own language, for the first three or four minutes I speak slower to allow the audience to tune in to my language and, of course, accent. I am sure you have experienced, when a foreigner speaks to you, the first two or three minutes of communication are the hardest while you tune in to their own accent or style of speaking.

While on this subject, you may have noticed that I have not talked about words such as 'er' and 'um' and I am not going to waste your reading time discussing them. They are not terribly important. If you have to 'er' and 'um', be enthusiastic with it. Change the level of your voice when giving an 'er' or an 'um', but certainly don't worry about it.

◀ *KEEP YOUR SPEECHES* ▶

The final good habit is to keep all your speeches. Always rewrite the text for each occasion, even though you may be speaking on exactly the same subject. The discipline of rewriting will help you to improve your presentation as well as refresh your memory and your subconscious mind.

When I say 'rewrite' I am not saying you have to create a new presentation, but do remember that at every presentation the audience is slightly different. You may be copying down exactly the same speech as you have given previously but, in the process, you will find you make one or two minor adjustments.

POCKET REMINDERS

- Use 'I' only sparingly
- 'We' and 'us' are good news words
- See things from the audience's point of view
- Never say that made-up stories are true
- Keep to your allotted time
- Don't worry about an accent or a stutter
- Keep all your speeches.

❻ **WISE WORDS** ❺

The essence of skill is extracting meaning from everyday experience.

Author unknown

10

Questions

◀ *ASKING THE AUDIENCE A* ▶
QUESTION

Before we deal with handling questions from the audience, let's first take the situation where a speaker asks the audience a question. Many speakers find that they don't get the reaction they were hoping for because they don't lead the audience into responding. For example, 'Ladies and gentlemen, how many of you came here by car?' Does the speaker want them to put their hand up or respond verbally? If the desired reaction is that they should raise their hands, the speaker should raise his or her hand in the air first.

So the speaker must always lead from the front. No doubt you recall the management principle: *When the leaders are leading, the followers will follow.*

◄ # QUESTION TIME ►

Now let's turn to the handling of questions from the audience. For many presenters, taking questions can be a harrowing experience. For others, it can become the most enjoyable part of their presentation. Therefore to make question time a success, it is important that the speaker establishes the ground rules.

Let's suppose the speaker doesn't want questions during the presentation. The speaker or the person that makes the introduction should make that clear at the beginning of the presentation. For example:

> Ladies and gentlemen, I anticipate there may be some points you wish to raise. We will therefore have time for questions at the end of my presentation, so please can you keep them until then.

If, on the other hand, the speaker doesn't want questions at all, how about this:

> Ladies and gentlemen, there may be some points you wish to raise at the conclusion of my presentation. I will be able to answer your questions personally on a one-to-one basis outside the scheduled proceedings, as I know some of you want to get away very quickly.

◄ ## TECHNIQUES FOR ► HANDLING QUESTIONS

If you are going to have a question session, there are some techniques that will help you to enjoy it and be confident in handling your audience.

The first technique is where you are asked the question and you in turn ask it straight back to the questioner. For example:

- 'I am sorry I didn't quite understand that,'
- 'Could you repeat that please?'
- 'I am not absolutely certain of your point. Could you explain exactly what you mean?'

There are a number of interesting facets to this technique. First, very rarely are questions repeated in exactly the same form and when repeated they are often made easier to answer. Secondly, some questions that appear to be difficult aren't questions but statements and the speaker can agree with or elaborate on that statement. Thirdly, and perhaps most importantly, by asking for the question to be repeated, the speaker is given some thinking time to come up with the answer.

IF YOU DON'T KNOW THE ANSWER

If it should happen that you don't know the answer to a question, never, and I really mean never, try to make up an answer. You should always say, 'I am sorry, I don't know the answer to that question,' and, depending on the importance of the question, you can say 'I will find out the answer for you' — and make sure you do.

Sometimes people who ask questions already know the answer. If you get it wrong you lose enormous credibility, apart from confidence and control, and it can devalue an otherwise superb presentation.

ASKING THE AUDIENCE

An extension of the previous technique is to ask your audience to help. You might be able to say, 'I am sorry, I don't know the answer to that question. Does anybody else know?' You will never lose respect from a person or an audience when you say, 'I am sorry, I don't know the answer to that.'

ELICITING QUESTIONS

Imagine that a speaker has planned a question session. They have set the ground rules for questions to be raised at the end of the presentation. The speaker then says, 'Ladies and gentlemen, we now have time for questions. I expect you've got many so let's have the first question please.'

The speaker has a big smile and has used the correct body language of moving from a standing position for presenting to a sitting position for question time. But no question is asked.

So the speaker says again, 'Let's have the first question please.' Still nothing happens. The smile now disappears from the speaker's face and he or she is possibly losing confidence rapidly. Now comes the final plea — and I mean it comes out as a plea — 'Well there must be some questions, surely somebody is going to ask one?'

Still no response. The audience is looking at their hands, they are very uncomfortable and one or two are trying desperately hard to think of a question.

So what should happen?

A properly prepared speaker who wants a question session to develop will themselves have ready three or four questions or prime one or two people to raise a question. Having asked the first time and possibly the second time without a response, the speaker will say, 'This is a question that is often asked of me' or 'This is a question that I was asked during the break'. Doing this normally gets a discussion under way and the speaker can turn to a member of the audience with a further question, 'How do you feel about that?' or 'What is your reaction to that?'

LOADED QUESTIONS

I am sure this will never happen to you but just in case it is best to be prepared so that you will know how to deal with it. What do you do if you are faced with a really nasty awkward loaded question?

It is easiest to explain the method of handling this type of question by creating a scenario.

Imagine you are the guest speaker at a particular public function. Your name has appeared on the publicity material and posters have gone up around town.

You must now imagine, and this is the difficult bit, that there is one person that really doesn't like you and this person, seeing that you are speaking at this function, believes that this is a golden opportunity to put you on the spot in public.

So the occasion arrives and you give, quite naturally, a fluent and excellent presentation. You now get to your question session and you have one or two nice questions to handle. Then suddenly out of the blue comes a really nasty question, normally from someone in the back row. That sort of questioner very rarely sits in the front.

So how do you handle that type of question?

Normally the first reaction will be that the colour drains from your cheeks and you glance towards the nearest exit. But what do you do? You must certainly not respond by attacking the questioner in an antagonistic fashion. For example, 'That's a downright unpleasant question. I've got no idea what right you think you have to say things like that.' The golden rule in maintaining audience empathy is that the speaker must never appear to attack a member of the audience.

The technique for handling the unpleasant questioner is really quite easy and in most cases very enjoyable. To be able to operate the technique you must first have an understanding of kinesics, which, as you know, is the technical term for body language, which I am sure you know is a very imprecise science.

There are approximately 700,000 body language signals. These are everything from facial expression, use of hands, posture, poise and body movements. As far as the spoken word is concerned, there are approximately 40,000 words and sounds that can be used. In northern Europe on a day-to-day basis we normally use about 4000. So whenever the body language information is in conflict with the verbal information, the body language signal is invariably correct. Most people can control what they say (not everybody can), but with 700,000 body language signals it is extremely difficult if not impossible to control that information.

I want to use one example of body language information that you need to understand to deal with the imaginary problem we have created. There is a zone of space approximately 18" around our body that is known as the intimate zone. It is space that is private and the only people we normally allow inside that space are people with whom we have a very close relationship. I am sure you have experienced a situation when somebody has come too close — if you are not on extremely personal terms with them you will back away.

There are also zones of space between the speaker and the audience that become comfortable zones. If a speaker moves from his or her speaking point towards someone while at the same time maintaining eye contact, this movement will inflict pressure on that individual.

Let's now return to the technique. On hearing that unpleasant question, the first thing to do is to smile. This will instantly relax your audience, as at this stage most audiences will experience embarrassment and the smile reassures them that you know exactly what you are doing.

You should then take a few paces towards the questioner, looking them straight in the eyes, leaning slightly forward and maintain a slight smile — not a wide grin. You ask your questioner the question back in the form that we have already discussed.

You will invariably find that when the question is repeated it will have changed and be in a completely different form from the original. You will have applied pressure without any verbal abuse.

HECKLERS

The heckler, on the other hand, is a completely different individual. Very rarely does a speaker have to cope with a heckler, and those who do are mostly politicians. You may experience the problem if you are an after-dinner speaker, particularly at very boozy company occasions where heckling the speaker is not only a great sport but the high point of the conference. There are of course many brilliant comedians who can generate a fast response and great repartee that can be extremely amusing.

If ever you are confronted and you are the sort of person that doesn't have an immediate witty response, get your audience to get you out of trouble.

The most important rule for all speakers is *never to lose your cool in front of an audience*. Your facial expression is crucial, so again you must always maintain a smile. You can respond to your heckler if you feel justified by saying that you will handle his or her point when the formal presentation has concluded. If the heckler continues to cause problems you can always say, 'Ladies and gentlemen, I do apologise about the amount of time this person is wasting on your behalf,' and then immediately move on to the next question or the delivery of your next speech. If necessary you can appeal to your audience for them to do something about it.

◀ NEVER LOSE CONTROL ▶

I must emphasise once again the importance of a speaker's facial expression, particularly a smile. And let me remind you again, it's not what you say but how you say it.

Try the following out on a friend.

First say without smiling, 'I think the speech you just gave was abysmal.' You will probably get a reaction of hostility, defensiveness and unpleasantness.

Now try the same phrase with a big smile. You will more than likely get the reaction, 'I totally agree with you, I thought it was awful too!'

Please do remember that it can be a great sport for an audience if the speaker loses control and starts to become uptight. If the speaker never appears to lose control and always maintains a positive, enthusiastic expression, she or he will always control the audience and their questions. As important as any technique in answering questions is to ensure the entire audience can hear the question. Always repeat the question loudly, and when answering, direct the answer to the questioner but make sure everyone can hear your reply.

POCKET REMINDERS

- Lead from the front
- Send difficult questions back
- Never make up an answer
- Prime someone to ask a question if necessary
- Never attack the questioner
- Keep smiling
- Never lose control.

❛ WISE WORDS ❜

An expert is a person who will know tomorrow why the things he predicted yesterday didn't happen today.

Author unknown

11

Function speaking

Function speaking is where you are invited to be the speaker at some event outside your normal environment.

Most people involved in public speaking are speaking either at client presentations or their own company events. The same principle nevertheless applies to events that you are in control of as well as those that you are not, and that is, of course, to be thoroughly prepared.

◀ *PREPARATION* ▶

Before writing your presentation for the function it is therefore essential that you are armed with the information that will help you to prepare correctly. How long are you expected to speak for? Where is the venue and what type of venue is it? Which part of the programme will you be speaking in? Who are the important people? What are they expecting you to deliver? Who will be speaking before and after you? What will they be talking about? How long is the whole event going to last?

You will also need to know and develop a full understanding of relevant titles and terminology that will of course help you to build audience identification and empathy. Many times otherwise faultless presentations have been ruined by the speaker addressing the delegates using incorrect terminology or, even worse, an incorrect title. For example, a speaker may call the attendees 'representatives' when their correct title is 'consultants'. I also like to have information about the people, their age levels, experience, guidance on salaries, their worries as well as their ambitions.

You will also need to know the purpose of the occasion. Is there a central theme? What is it? What do they want you to call your presentation or what are you going to call it?

All this can be summed up by suggesting that you make sure you receive a thorough brief and ask as many questions as you possibly can.

◀ *ON ARRIVAL* ▶

Some well-known personalities, who have heavy time constraints, arrive at a function just a few minutes before they are due to speak. I don't know how they get away with it and very few of them are able to get the reaction that they should.

My own belief is that it is extremely rude not to arrive well before the event starts and I recommend that every speaker should be there right from the beginning so that they can hear what has been said before their own presentation. They will be able to soak up the atmosphere and they can also be reminded of terminology, points of interest and detail.

Apart from anything else, arriving early makes sense because it enables you to check the room layout, microphone strength, lighting, distractions behind the presentation area, and to check through or, even better, rehearse your visual aids.

◀ *VENUE* ▶

The room layout can have a direct effect on the speaker's method of delivery. People are more relaxed, their minds are more likely to be receptive and they will be more responsive when they are seated close together. We have all attended a seminar or theatre that has not been full and we know that our own appreciation is not as great as if every seat had been taken.

If you can play any part in the seating arrangements, always make sure that the front rows are filled first. Always put less chairs in than the numbers expected to attend and do attempt to fill every empty space. Then if everybody does turn up there is a feeling of excitement as extra chairs have to be put out, which will give the feeling that this event must be worth attending because it is full.

You must check to make sure that there are no distractions immediately behind the position where you are going to speak from. Some venues have a huge mirror, others have windows, others may have a picture, all of which should be removed or covered if possible.

I am sure you will have seen some political events where there are a number of well-known personalities cluttered around the speaker. They can become a distraction.

Similar to this are occasions where you are requested to speak from behind the top table. Do try and avoid this. I personally will never speak from behind a top table and will very rarely allow anybody else on a platform from which I am to make a presentation.

Imagine the scene — the top table, a guest speaker, a managing director, a financial director and a sales director. The MD has finished his presentation. The guest speaker is now presenting. Let's see what is happening.

The managing director isn't listening because he is thinking about all the things he left out of his speech. The financial director isn't listening because he's crossing out of his speech all the things the MD just spoke about. The sales director is not listening because more than likely he is writing his talk there and then because he never has enough time.

So the audience looking at the top table see these very important people not really concentrating and they don't concentrate either. That is why it is so important for speakers not to be seen until they are giving their presentation.

If you have the chance to influence seating arrangements, you will get a far better reaction from an audience seated classroom style (behind tables) than theatre style (without tables). Being able to ease your weight onto your elbows is more comfortable and the table provides a feeling of security.

◀ INTRODUCING THE SPEAKER ▶

Finally, the speaker introduction must be stage-managed. When making a presentation to an unfamiliar audience it is normal for the speaker to be introduced by the chairman or the MC of the event and it is the speaker's responsibility to make sure that the introduction is not only factually correct but is also designed to get the desired reaction. It is perfectly acceptable for the introducer to build the speaker up to the audience by explaining his or her credentials, experience and right to speak on the subject.

The purpose of all this, apart from establishing credibility, is also to diminish the chance of the speaker introducing themselves and falling into the trap of the 'I' syndrome. But the introduction is best written by the speaker or at least the key points drafted and presented to the introducer.

These introductions can so easily go wrong.

I once heard a chairman introducing his guest speaker, 'Ladies and gentlemen, I am indeed very honoured to welcome our esteemed guest here today. He is recognised as one of the world's authorities on um, um, er, er, er ...'

Searching among his papers in a deathly hush with the esteemed guest changing colour and twitching in his chair, the chairman located his briefing note and soldiered on. 'I know, ladies and gentlemen, that we are all going to benefit by having this opportunity to hear his experience and gain from his knowledge. So, without further ado, let me introduce you to er, um, um, er, er, er ...'

The chairman leant over to the speaker who whispered his name to the chairman, but the latter was slightly hard of hearing and proceeded to mispronounce the esteemed guest's name.

POCKET REMINDERS

- Be thoroughly prepared
- Arrive early
- Check out the venue
- Avoid distractions
- Write your own introduction.

WISE WORDS

You can't build a reputation on what you're going to do.

Henry Ford

12

Visual Aids

Microphones seem to be held in particular awe by the inexperienced. I am sure you have seen speakers who walk to the microphone, look at it as if it is going to bite them, lean towards it and blow at it. Or those who speak to it by bellowing 'Is it on?' and continue to test its performance by thumping it over the head which of course, if it is on, deafens the audience.

More experienced speakers will check the sound equipment long before the audience is present. As a guideline, and to be on the safe side, about 80 per cent of all venues will not have perfectly functioning equipment, although they will claim that they do.

Arriving early enables you to check. Do remember that spare parts are difficult to obtain after 4 pm.

To test a microphone, just count up to ten in a normal voice. It seems that so many otherwise fluent individuals suddenly dry up when requested to test the microphone. To get the level right in the room or hall, always remember that you will need more volume when the room is full.

The best sort of microphone to use is one that is fastened to your lapel or tie or suspended around your neck. This of course enables you to move. If you are faced with only a fixed microphone on the stand you must, of course, not move away. I have occasionally in desperation suspended a rather bulky microphone around my neck with a bootlace or piece of string, taking care to cover the bottom half of the microphone with some insulating tape so that its movement would not pick up the rustle of my clothes.

◀ LIGHTING ▶

Lighting is an important part of a good presentation as the speaking area should always be well lit and the speaker's face must be clearly seen. Again, another reason for arriving early is to make sure that the lighting is correct.

Many events require the audience to be put into darkness to allow back screen projectors or slides to illustrate the presentation. It makes it very difficult for speakers to communicate effectively if the audience is in the dark. If you are able to influence the organiser, do try to make sure that there is some lighting on your audience.

◀ FLIP-CHARTS AND ▶ CHALKBOARDS

The various visual aids available to most speakers start with a chalkboard or flip-chart. I have already pointed out that they should be positioned one pace from the speaker's presentation point. If the speaker is right-handed, visual aids should be positioned on the left-hand side and vice versa, as this will reduce excessive and unnecessary movement.

I have heard it said that you should not turn your back on an audience, but it is difficult to write without doing that. I really don't think that it is particularly important as long as the speaker, if he or she is not facing the audience, keeps up a flow of conversation. If the conversation ceases, this does break the relationship that should have been built up with the audience.

If you are going to show previously prepared information on a flip-chart, it must be professionally done or look of high quality. A speaker can get away with bad writing or extraordinary diagrams if they are being created in front of the audience.

When preparing a flip-chart, always avoid the top three inches as in turning the sheets over this can often be obliterated. And finally, check that the flip-chart or whiteboard can be clearly seen from all parts of the audience.

◄ *OVERHEAD PROJECTORS* ►

Make sure that the overhead projector (OHP) you are using has a good light output and a spare bulb, and that it is focused correctly with the image filling the screen and not spilling off onto the back walls.

If you are going to use previously prepared transparencies, they should look professional. It is not necessary to keep switching the projector off and on to change transparencies. The time to switch it off is when you are not using it. Continually switching an OHP off and on can be very annoying for any audience and it is particularly frustrating if the speaker can't find the on and off switch. Always when putting a transparency on the OHP glance back to the screen to make sure it is positioned correctly and not at an angle. Always remove any visual from your audience's view if you are not currently speaking about it.

Previously prepared material, whether in the form of a flip-chart, OHP transparency or a slide, should contain a minimum of detail. Far too many speakers cram too much information onto their visuals. It is much more effective, if you have to communicate facts and figures, for them to be on a printed handout than on a visual that the audience has difficulty in seeing and then is removed too quickly before the information can be assimilated.

SLIDES

Slide projection, from the front or the back, gives the speaker an even greater opportunity to back up the spoken material with visual emphasis. Everything from photography to cartoons, bar charts to statements can be included. At some events the speaker will not be in control as the slides will be moved when appropriate by a conference organiser. At these events the speaker must of course rehearse the presentation to make sure that the key words enabling the controller to move the slides are clear. Other events provide the opportunity for the speaker to move the slides with either a remote control button or through a control switch on the lectern.

In either case the speaker must always check not only that the slides are in the right order, but that they are the right way up and the right way round, as well as being in focus. The technology for presentations is moving at such a rate that it is now in fairly wide use that computer generated slides and images can be created in a matter of minutes and produced straight onto a large conference screen. This allows the latest information as well as final last minute changes to take place.

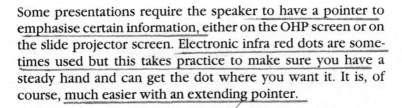

POINTERS

Some presentations require the speaker to have a pointer to emphasise certain information, either on the OHP screen or on the slide projector screen. Electronic infra red dots are sometimes used but this takes practice to make sure you have a steady hand and can get the dot where you want it. It is, of course, much easier with an extending pointer.

Though it is not a visual aid, the autocue or teleprompter must be discussed. We have all seen it achieve far greater exposure through the major politicians of the world. We have seen the politicians who use this communication aid effectively and those who seem to be showing the whites of their eyes to the audience while their eyeball is on the autocue and their face is going towards a section of the audience. The use of this equipment must, of course, be practised. A variety of skills are required. The tendency to simply read the script while moving ones face is not getting the best from this aid.

At many in-company conferences or events, the speaker has to use the prompter in a darkened environment. We have already discussed the lack of merit of this procedure. But whether in the dark or in a well-lit hall, autocue gives the speaker a greater chance to maximise the 'how you say it' rather than concentrating on what is said. It is certainly more comfortable for an audience to have the presenter looking at them rather than downwards at their prepared text or notes.

The disadvantage of this controlled method of delivery is that it can never be as exciting, enthusiastic or passionate as the presenter who uses the methodology I have outlined in this book. So like all the other visual aids and like everything else about public speaking, preparation and practice do prevent disasters.

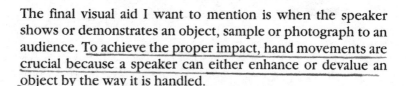

The final visual aid I want to mention is when the speaker shows or demonstrates an object, sample or photograph to an audience. To achieve the proper impact, hand movements are crucial because a speaker can either enhance or devalue an object by the way it is handled.

Hold the object at least at shoulder height, handle it as if it were a piece of beautiful Waterford crystal, keep your hands and fingers open and make sure that all the members of the audience can see it clearly.

POCKET REMINDERS

- Test all equipment
- If you have to turn your back on the audience, keep talking
- All visuals must look professional
- Preparation and practice prevent disasters.

WISE WORDS

You can make more friends in two months by becoming interested in other people than you can in two years by trying to get the other person interested in you.

Dale Carnegie

Summary

I hope by now I have removed any mystique from the very simple subject of public speaking. Most of the ideas contained in *Speak for Yourself* are common sense but, as we all know, common sense is not too common.

There is no incredible magic formula. It really is very straight-forward.

Great speakers enjoy speaking. They deliver with enthusiasm. Their audiences are infected with their enthusiasm and their speaking occasions are events to look forward to.

This doesn't happen overnight. Like every element of personal development, it is reached one stage at a time.

For further books or information on Richard Denny, as well as personal development audio cassettes and video training pro-grammes, contact:

The Richard Denny Organisation
PO Box 16
Moreton in Marsh
Gloucestershire
GL56 0NH

YES YOU CAN BE A GREAT SPEAKER

If you think you are beaten you are,
If you think you dare not you don't,
If you like to win, but think you can't
It is almost certain that you won't.

Life's battles don't always go to the
stronger or faster person, but sooner
or later the person who wins is
the person who thinks they can.

GOOD LUCK AND GREAT SPEAKING

The final checklist

This book is obviously written to help those who would like to be more persuasive and confident communicators. As has been previously stated, this quite naturally does not happen overnight. Please use the following checklists regularly as they will help dramatically with any planned improvement. The final checklist is your own critical analysis to use after each presentation. You can, of course, get other people's reactions, particularly to posture, voice control and facial expression. Do not judge yourself too harshly, but be fair and finally let me remind you once again: preparation builds your confidence and enthusiasm creates the inspirational delivery.

◀ ## *CHECK OUT YOUR* ▶
PREPARATION □

- Have I researched my subject? □

- Have I a system for collating ideas? □

- Have I decided the required reaction? □

- Have I checked to see what reaction is expected? □

- Do I have a logical sequence? □

- Have I prepared my speaking aid/notes □

◀ ## *CHECK OUT YOUR PRESENTATION* ☐ ▶

- Are my opening words attention-getting? ☐

- Do I have one or more people stories? ☐

- Have I created audience acceptance? ☐

- Am I selling the results of my message? ☐

- Have I checked the length of my presentation? ☐

- Will my content be clearly understood? ☐

- Am I sure I am not covering too many points? ☐

- Have I avoided too many detailed facts and figures? ☐

- Have I created an effective close to my presentation? ☐

◀ *CHECK OUT YOURSELF* ☐ ▶

- Am I feeling confident? ☐

- Am I looking forward to my delivery? ☐

- Do I feel enthusiastic? ☐

- Do I look the part – hair/clothes etc? ☐

- Am I positively seeing in my mind a successful result? ☐

- Have I discarded all negative thoughts? ☐

- Am I feeling physically fit and well? ☐

- Am I going to smile sometimes? ☐

- Will I look in the mirror before speaking? ☐

◀ ## CHECK OUT YOUR DELIVERY □ ▶

- Have I checked the venue? □

- Have I checked the equipment? □

- Have I checked the layout? □

- Do I know who will be speaking before me? □

- Have I checked how I will be introduced? □

- Am I prepared to stop when my time is up? □

- Have I prepared a question session (if applicable)? □

- Have I prepared my pauses/loud voice/soft voice? □

- Can my visuals clearly be seen and understood by everyone? □

- Can I be heard? □

- Can I be seen clearly? □

Check the improvements

After each presentation, get into the habit of de-briefing your-self. Think back through your presentation and pick out areas where you feel there could be improvements. As well as that, re-live the good moments. Recall audience reaction on various points that you raised. Now mark yourself out of 10 on the items listed below and then next time you are going to make a presentation, actively work on the item with the lowest mark:

◀ ## CHECK THE IMPROVEMENTS ▶

DATE

- Start ☐ ☐ ☐ ☐ ☐

- Enthusiasm ☐ ☐ ☐ ☐ ☐

- Posture ☐ ☐ ☐ ☐ ☐

- Facial expression ☐ ☐ ☐ ☐ ☐

- Voice control ☐ ☐ ☐ ☐ ☐

- Picture power ☐ ☐ ☐ ☐ ☐

- People stories ☐ ☐ ☐ ☐ ☐

- Content ☐ ☐ ☐ ☐ ☐

- Did I sell it? ☐ ☐ ☐ ☐ ☐

- The finish ☐ ☐ ☐ ☐ ☐

Total

◀ *MONEY BACK GUARANTEE** ▶

I am so positive that if you apply the techniques from this book you will increase your persuasive and communication skills and that if you are not satisfied, I will give you your money back.

* Return this book together with your purchase receipt within 30 days of purchase to:

Richard Denny
PO Box 16
Moreton-in-Marsh
Gloucestershire
GL56 0NH